CHI CHI'S SECRETS
OF POWER GOLF

CHI CHI'S SECRETS

OF **POWER** GOLF

by JUAN (CHI CHI) RODRIGUEZ

NEW YORK / THE VIKING PRESS

I dedicate this book to my second father, Ed Dudley.

If it had not been for him, I would never have had a chance to play professional golf.

God bless his memory.

C O N T E N T S

I put my whole body into each shot. As a fellow pro said, "left side, right side, all of it."

A solid stroking position before impact helps to overcome other faults.

INTRODUCTION

The most powerful swing in golf today belongs to one of the smallest members of the Professional Golfer's Association — Juan "Chi Chi" Rodriguez.

Chi Chi Rodriguez is 5 feet 7. He weighs 120 pounds and he consistently drives a golf ball between 270 and 300 yards. He has been so successful since he changed his stance and his grip four years ago that he is one of the leading money winners on the PGA tour and is regarded as one of the game's better players.

"But," he says, "four years ago I could not hit the ball out of my shadow." What transformed him? Fellow pro Bob Toski has an interesting analysis. "Chi Chi Rodriguez," he said, "does not adhere to all the fundamentals of a perfectly formful golf swing. However, this tremendous power hitter does overcome his faults by moving into a solid stroking position before impact."

Mason Rudolph, another touring professional, has a similar analysis. "He has a way of getting everything into a shot," Rudolph said. "When he turns that 'secret' loose, he's getting his whole body into the ball, left side, right side, all of it."

The secret to Chi Chi's game is what he calls the perfectly solid left wall. "This," he said, "is where all the power comes from. This is what I developed three years ago. It is not very difficult to learn this theory. Any golfer, large or small, male or female, can utilize it to improve his or her game. But let me caution against too much change, especially if the

The solid left side is where I develop my power. This is my "secret." Without it, I would not be successful. I call this the left-wall principle.

change isn't natural. Also the individual must not expect that my moves will suit his. There are many different steps to building the left wall, and there are many steps involved in correct execution. Only practice will help you develop this.

"The important factor is not to break the wall in any manner. Because if you do, you consequently ruin your follow-through and your swing. Essentially, this is my game because I use the fundamentals of the wall on nearly every shot."

The solid left side, most professionals agree, is a must for a successful golf game. "It is impossible," says Dai Rees, "or nearly impossible, to find a golfer who hits against the left side playing really bad golf. True, he may have other faults, but if his left side is as it ought to be then he is very definitely on the right road. This hitting against the left side is not just an isolated part of the swing.

"On the contrary, it is an integral part of it and should be regarded as such. I would ask you to pay a great deal of attention to it, because the braced left side is what I call the final payoff. Your grip, your stance, your taking the club back, might all be just what is required, but if the left side collapses then all is lost."

This book, then, will dwell primarily on the wall and the proper grip, stance, and swings to make it work correctly. But the other aspects of the game have not been forgotten. Chi Chi also has some valuable tips on putting, iron and wood play, trouble shots, and the mental outlook needed in golf.

"Remember," Chi Chi says, "golf is a game of confidence,

but to gain that confidence you must perfect dozens of details.
In my case, the development of an immovable left side
aided the other parts of my game. And the more confidence I
had in my long shots, the more confidence I gained in
other aspects."

SANDY PADWE

CHI CHI'S SECRETS OF POWER GOLF

The straight left wall begins at the top of the left shoulder and continues to the left foot.

THE LEFT-WALL THEORY

Generating Power

When I was caddying as a youngster in Puerto Rico, I watched the professionals constantly, picking up every tip I could, trying it, then either using it if it suited me or discarding it if it didn't. I followed the same pattern when I turned professional. I watched constantly, learning, experimenting.

The one professional who always made an impression on me was Dr. Cary Middlecoff. I played with him as often as I could, and the part of his game that I always remembered was the way he built his power around his left side.

When I changed my style a few years ago, I kept Middlecoff in mind. I was looking for more power and I found it because I learned to build a solid wall of my left side, a wall that would not move under any circumstances.

The theory is, if I have a strong left side and can hit against it, then I can develop a lot of power. At 120 pounds, I need all the power I can find because I have a big family to feed.

This straight left wall begins at the top of the left shoulder and continues to the left foot. When I say straight, I mean it literally. The worry is not about my head or my hands, but about the body. It should be perfectly vertical.

Special Exercises

I used to do special isometric exercises to help build this left side. I would go home and stand with my left shoulder, hip, leg, and foot directly against a door frame. Then I would exert isometric pressure to build the muscles on my left side.

Another exercise consisted of placing an imaginary club in my right hand. I would take an imaginary backswing, then the downswing. And always during these swings I concentrated on keeping the entire left side of my body perfectly straight. I also made sure all points of that side touched and never left the door frame. The idea was to practice so much that keeping that solid left wall became almost as natural as inserting the car key into the ignition.

There is only one way to develop this wall, and that is through constant practice and exercise. As you will learn, everything evolves from being perfectly straight on all your shots that require power.

Positioning the Feet

As you are practicing, you will begin to notice that you are
starting to dig your right foot into the surface of the turf.
You dig in with the inside of the sole of your right shoe. This
is very important because digging your right foot gives you the
thrust and power you need for distance hitting.

The positioning of the left foot is extremely important, too.
At the conclusion of the swing, in the case of the smaller
golfer, the left foot should be pointing to your right. In other
words, it must be slightly pigeon-toed. If you move your
left foot, the whole left side of the wall moves out of
position and you make a poor shot.

I cannot stress this point too much, for smaller golfers.
During the downswing the left foot serves as a brace. If the
brace breaks, so does the swing. For the normal-sized
golfer, I recommend that the left foot remain straight or very
slightly turned to the left.

*At the conclusion of the swing,
especially for the small golfer,
the left foot must be slightly
pigeon-toed. If you move your
left foot, the wall will collapse.*

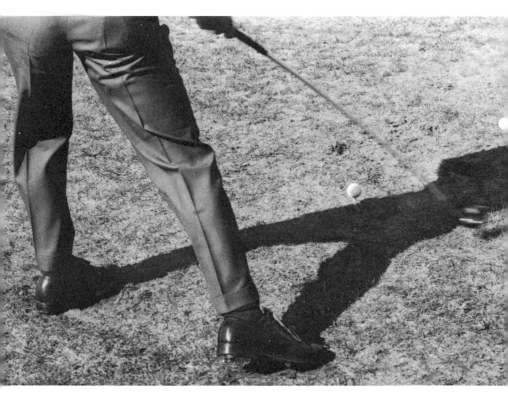

*The left foot serves as a brace.
If the brace breaks, so does the
swing.*

Feel Natural

There is no one thing that gives me my power. It is a
combination of many difficult moves, and these moves must
all become secondary and eventually feel natural.

From experience, I recommend only what is most
comfortable. This is a very important point. Too many golfers
read too many books and try to go out and do exactly what
the words say. This is a mistake. Books can be used only as a
general guide. I suggest experimentation with the three
main grips: the overlapping, the interlocking, and the baseball.
After trying the three, I found the overlapping most
comfortable and most suitable for my game.

Stance is equally important. I instruct my pupils at Dorado
Beach to keep the feet the same distance apart as the width of
the shoulders. A stance like that will not restrict a full
shoulder and hip turn.

When you have found your proper grip and stance, then
you are ready to begin perfecting the left wall. And when you
have sufficiently built the wall, then it is time to adapt the
rest of your game to this theory. But the wall is the key.
Always remember that. A strong one eliminates the biggest
problem in golf — body sway.

Be Comfortable

The most important factor in a grip is that it should be completely comfortable for the individual. I can't stress that enough. Too many people use the wrong grip — for all too many of the wrong reasons.

I use the overlapping grip because it happens to suit me best and helps me control my club better. But I'm not telling everybody who reads this book that the overlapping grip is a must for a powerful golf swing. The best grip is one which leads to a smooth swing. It is that simple.

I have very small, narrow hands and short fingers. I use the overlapping grip because I feel my hands work better as a unit. This helps in overcoming a lack of natural power. When I tell people I have little strength in my hands, fingers, and wrists, they usually give me an unbelieving stare. But it is true.

Overlapping Grip

In the overlapping (also called the Vardon) grip, the little finger of the right hand overlaps the left index finger.

Generally speaking, the overlapping is a good grip for most golfers. It is especially good for beginners because it is easy to learn. It also feels natural to most beginners, and comfort, as I have emphasized, is of the utmost importance.

This grip, when used correctly, holds the hands together

In the overlapping grip, the little finger of the right hand overlaps the left index finger.

in such a manner that there is no way the club can move in the palm of the hand. If the club moves in the palm of the hand, the result is usually a bad shot.

In my grip, the left thumb and hand are well on top of the shaft and the hands are securely joined for fine control. The V (between the thumb and index finger) on my left hand points between my right shoulder and my head. The V on my right hand points to my chin. If both Vs are pointing at the right shoulder it will cause a hook. The grip is firm, but not too tight.

Sam Snead always says the golf swing is like hitting a baseball. "If you squeeze the bat to death," he says, "and use all your power throughout the swing, you put less power into the ball at contact. You want to let that power go when you hit the ball. You not only hit it farther, you swing smoother because you're relaxed."

In my left hand, the club runs diagonally across the palm with the fingers wrapping around. In my right hand I hold the club handle across the middle joint of my fingers. My right thumb is slightly on the left side of the club handle and my left thumb fits into the pocket formed between the right side of the club handle and the palm of my right hand. I grip the club more firmly with the left hand than with the right, and I concentrate on making this left-hand grip firm.

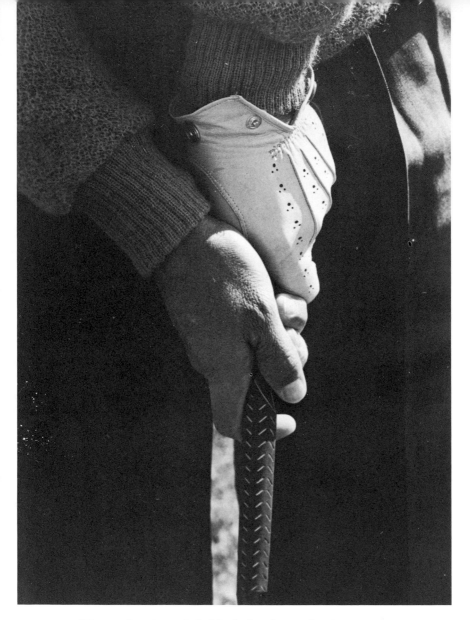

The overlapping grip holds the hands together in such a way that the club will not move.

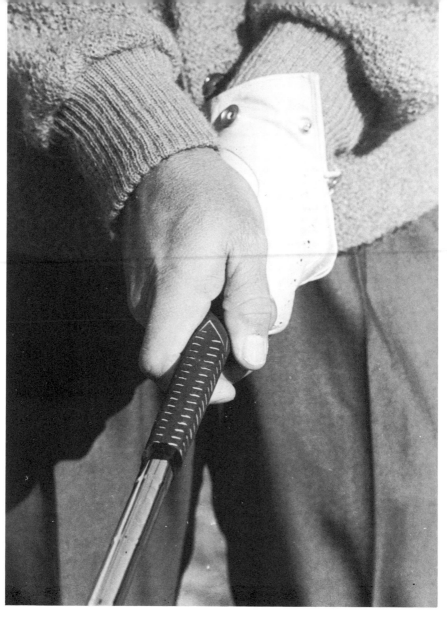

In my grip the left thumb and hand are well on top of the shaft.

I concentrate on gripping the club more firmly with the left hand.

Interlocking and Baseball Grips

If the overlapping grip isn't comfortable, then try the
interlocking, which is a combination palm and finger grip.
The pressure of the right hand is in the first two fingers and
the thumb. The right hand's little finger interlocks with
the forefinger of the left. Keep the hands close together for
power and control.

Another grip is the baseball. Its name is self-explanatory.
You just grip the club as you would grip a baseball bat. It is
called the ten-finger grip because you put all the fingers
on the club. The thumb of the left hand rests in the palm of the
right hand. This increases holding power on the club because
it places all the fingers on the shaft. But it does not unify
the two hands.

It took me years — thirteen, to be exact — before I came up
with the right grip. Previously I had used an interlocking
grip; when I changed I kept saying to myself, "I can't play golf
like this." But with practice and more practice I was able
to overcome my fears and develop a good grip. It can
be the same with you.

I use a slightly open stance. My right foot is about an inch beyond my shoulder.

STANCE

Enough Body Turn Is Essential

There is only one way to generate the speed you need for power and that is by having the proper stance before you even attempt to swing the club. Again, the prime factor in selecting a stance has to be complete comfort. But there is another factor: which stance will allow you the biggest body turn?

Main Stances

There are three main stances — the square, the closed, and the open. In the square stance you place your feet directly along the intended line of flight of your shot. Point the toes slightly out and be sure you distribute your weight evenly between both feet.

In the closed stance, the main difference is that you drop the right foot slightly back from the intended line of flight of the shot. This, in effect, causes the hips and body to swing slightly to the right.

In the open stance your left foot is slightly drawn back from the intended line of flight, causing the hips and body to face slightly to the left.

I use a slightly open stance, drawing my left foot back a bit from the imaginary line. My right foot is about an inch or so beyond the outside of my right shoulder. This is fine for smaller men like myself who use a lot of leg movement and need maximum stability.

It took me a long time to decide on this position, but when I finally did I realized it was the one that allowed me the biggest body turn. For the average golfer, though, I suggest a stance where the feet are no farther apart than are the shoulders. Anything wider might restrict a full shoulder and hip turn.

After you have experimented sufficiently and have decided on the proper footing, you can complete the rest of your stance. While addressing the ball, flex the knees slightly. This helps you distribute the weight of the feet toward the heel instead of toward the ball of the foot. When you have your weight properly distributed, and your knees are flexed slightly, you should have a feeling that you are sitting down at the ball.

Positioning the Left Foot

This brings me to an essential point in my stance, a point which has the greatest bearing on the success of the left wall. This is the positioning of the left foot. How many times, while I have been giving lessons back home at Dorado Beach, have I seen a golfer turn his left foot toward the hole during the swing? This is especially bad for the small man like myself who swings very hard on the downswing.

I admit my left foot is in a very unusual position because I point it one-half turn to the right. It appears that I am pigeon-toed when I do this. But understand my reasoning. Because of my very hard downswing, my left foot has to serve as a brace. It keeps me from losing my balance and actually falling. Without the iron left side, there would be nothing to arrest the turning of the hips, and subsequently I would get a hook.

But remember, I recommend the pigeon-toed left foot mainly for small men. A large man has a naturally long arc, and he can take a narrow stance which will help him turn easily into his backswing. He doesn't have to make the same effort the small man does to get clubhead speed. But now I am getting into another area, which I will cover thoroughly in the next chapter. My swing is probably the most essential part of my game, with the exception of the left-wall principle.

Your left foot keeps you from losing your balance.

Without a strong left side, there would be nothing to prevent you from getting a hook.

Right Knee, Head, and Eyes

Before moving on, I would like to add a few comments about
the position of my right knee in my stance, and the position
of my head and eyes.

Many people have commented and noticed the exaggerated
right knee bend I use during the address. The knee is
actually bent toward the left leg. This is not a must for power
golf. It is just something I developed in searching for my
most comfortable stance.

As for the head and the eyes, I always keep my head about
six inches in back of the ball at address and tilted slightly
to the right. I concentrate on looking at the ball with my left
eye and I keep this eye on the ball throughout my entire
backswing and downswing.

It is a fallacy that the head must remain absolutely still
on each shot. This is almost physically impossible. But
you have to concentrate on keeping it as still as possible on
every shot. As Cary Middlecoff says, "The head is the
gyroscope of the entire swing, so far as balance is concerned."

My feet are slightly farther apart than my shoulders.

SWING

Always Experiment

Everything I have related thus far has been a buildup for the most important factor that contributes to the power I generate. While the principle of the wall is the basis for everything, my swing, unorthodox as it is, makes the ball travel 270 to 300 yards each time. My swing may not be picture-pretty, but it enables me to coil enormous power in my body, which I release when I hit the ball. It is a swing that confounds the purists because most of the things I do are wrong. But I still get results, my own way. This is why I have said repeatedly that experimentation is so important in determining what is most comfortable.

Backswing

Now, from the beginning, let me analyze my swing and the movements that make it smooth.

At address, my left arm is extended and relatively relaxed. My right arm is completely relaxed and tucked in to the side. My right shoulder is lower than the left. My feet are positioned slightly farther apart than the shoulders.

On the backswing, I use a slow turn. I don't particularly concentrate on taking the club back with the hands. I just think of a good 45-degree-angle turn of the shoulders and hips. My body, during the backswing, is moving laterally off the

*I use a slow turn on the backswing, thinking of a
good angle turn of the shoulders and hips.*

ball, to the right. Principally, this increases the distance the clubhead travels on the backswing and gives me the arc of a much bigger man. Because of this, I naturally get more club velocity.

I also take the club back very low to the ground so when I come back I flatten the path of the clubhead through the ball. I accomplish this by bending the knees and turning my legs during the backswing, more than is customary for the average golfer. When the club has reached the top of the backswing, I am in a semi-crouch.

By now, my left knee has moved well to the right of the ball and I eventually come off my left heel — much more so than a bigger man does. This additional leg turn is essential in my swing, however, allowing me to coil the muscles in my right thigh and reach for the fullest extension possible of the left arm and the muscles of the upper back. This, then, is where I generate the power in my downswing.

When the club has reached the top of the backswing,
I am in a semi-crouch.

Downward Movement

The down movement is the most important part of my swing. When I have reached the desired height of the backswing, I pause slightly. With my backswing completed, I am braced and crouched. My shoulder turn is now about 90 degrees, but the hips turn much less. My left heel is higher off the ground than is usual for golfers. I then start the downswing with a tremendous pull of my left hand. It may appear that I am trying to hit the ball with the bottom part of the club held in the left hand.

But about halfway down, things change. I throw my right shoulder as hard and fast as possible into the shot, with a sweeping motion. Now it appears that I am trying to hit the ball with my right shoulder alone. This hard swing-through with my right shoulder is not just a fast, jerking motion. It is part of my complete, smooth downswing.

I pause slightly when I reach the height of my back-swing.

*It may appear that I am trying to hit the ball with
the bottom part of the club held in the left hand.*

I throw my right shoulder as hard and fast as possible into the shot . . .

. . . and continue with a sweeping motion.

At this point I am also using my legs to the fullest extent. When I start back toward the ball, my left heel has been slammed back into the ground. Note also that I keep my wrists cocked as I start down. Then I drive laterally into the ball with a combination of the forceful movement of the left arm, the right shoulder, and the muscles in the right thigh.

These are the muscles I spoke of in the backswing, the muscles that were fully wound up at the top of my back movement. Now I use them for power, and the power pushes me forward. Halfway down, my knees are wider apart as I brace my lower body to withstand the impact shock. The wrists still are cocked, and the left arm is straight. My right elbow has returned to my side.

Impact

On impact, my right arm extends as I hit the ball. My left foot gives way to tremendous unwinding action. My left shoulder moves up rapidly, showing a very pronounced tilt and turn of the shoulders. By now, my weight has moved well off the right side, which is normal since the clubhead has moved through the ball and started up. My hips, shoulders, and knees are turning at their greatest momentum at this point. My head position shows that I don't let it restrict my swing. Although the clubhead has struck the ball only a second earlier, my head has turned so that I am looking down the fairway.

By impact, my weight has moved well off the right side.

Extremely important now is that my left leg is still braced so it can absorb the force of the swing. The wall is strong. It has not crumpled. Whew! Even talking about it tires me out, and I am violating my philosophy on golf. I would not want the average golfer to think of all those things when he is swinging. He would probably wind up missing the ball.

Concentration on Shoulder and Hip Turn

What you should do is apply and try some of the rules. See if they work for you. Then practice. It is the only way to improve the swing and get the power you need. If you are going to keep one thing in mind when you start the backswing, concentrate on getting the good turn of the shoulders and hips.

Also keep in mind that you are inviting trouble by starting the downswing with a hard pull or thrust of the right arm only. Start the downswing with a tremendous pull of the left hand. By doing it with the right, you cause the wrists to break or uncock near the top of the downswing. This causes a loss of power by the time the clubhead reaches the ball. The initial right-arm pull also can cause you to lose your correct aim. The result is usually a drastic hook to the left or a bad slice to the right.

The wall remains strong. It has not crumpled.

W O O D S

The Power Clubs

Used correctly with the left-wall principle, the woods, your distance clubs, will bring you the yardage necessary to lower your golf score. Actually, there is not much difference between your wood swing and your medium-iron swing except that with the woods you're putting more into it.

Of course the driver is the biggest weapon in my bag. This is the club that puts the steak in my mouth. Speaking of steak, I will always remember the Denver Open of 1963, which I won with a 276. I attribute the low score, in part, to consistent wood play. For example, on a 590-yard par-5 hole, I used a driver and a 4-wood and wound up 20 feet from the cup after two strokes. In the Buick Open that same year I had a double eagle on another par-5 hole. But it rained later, and the tournament officials canceled the round and my double eagle.

Body Speed Is Essential

I have discussed thoroughly the swing and stance needed for gaining the maximum distance and power, so I will confine myself now to some tips about uses of the woods. First, I concentrate on speeding my legs, knees, and hands. Body speed is essential for the small man.

There is no reason why you can't acquire speed. If you can dance, you can work on a speedier golf swing. It just takes concentration and work, plenty of it. You should not, however, sacrifice smoothness for speed. You need them both to get off a good drive.

Added Distance

As I have mentioned before, I always keep my driver low to the ground when I begin the backswing, so that when I come back I can get the whole club into the ball. There are other ways to obtain added distance. Gary Player had a novel idea. He had his clubs made one-half inch longer than the standard length he had been using. Why? Well, longer clubs give a longer swing arc. The longer the arc, the longer the shot will carry.

A tip to keep in mind when you're driving is to tee up the ball as high as the tee will allow. This is the only advantage you get in golf; you might as well make the best of it.

High and Low Shots

On hitting high and low shots, I do many different things. By high shots, I mean ones that must carry trees, water hazards, or sand traps. When I want to hit a high shot, I place my feet wider apart. This makes me shorten my backswing. The shorter the backswing, the higher I hit the ball. The reason I hit higher is because my weight is on the right foot longer.

When I want to hit low, I put my feet closer together. This gives me longer arc, longer backswing. In a situation like this I also keep the weight on the left foot. During the downswing this will help to keep the clubhead closer to the ground. On low shots I also play the ball a little farther back toward the right foot. I hit down and through the ball with a minimum of wrist action.

Wind Shots

The wind can be a crucial factor in your final score, so you must know how to hit against the wind or with it. When you're playing a low shot against the wind, tilt the tee forward and play the ball farther back toward the middle. This will give the ball a lower trajectory, for less wind resistance. You should not swing harder on a shot like this, but easier.

When you are playing with the wind, tilt the tee backward and play the ball slightly forward. This will give the ball

I keep my driver low to the ground. It helps me get the whole club into the ball.

The 3-wood, the fairway club, gives you distance
and height.

a higher trajectory, allowing the wind to give the ball greater distance. Again, don't hit harder.

Crosswind shots can be tricky. Play these shots normally and adjust your direction rather than attempt a compensating hook or slice. If the wind is very heavy, select the club next higher than the one you normally would use.

Using the Woods

Briefly, now, let's go into the use of the 2-, 3-, 4-, and 5-woods. The brassie, or No. 2 wood, is an excellent woman's club for use off the tee. Beginners and women usually have trouble getting the ball up. This club has added loft and helps them with this phase of the game. Its distance is about 200 yards. Using the brassie in the fairway is inadvisable unless the ball is in an exceptionally good position — as Julius Boros says, "staring you in the eye."

The 3-wood, or spoon, is the main fairway club. It is a distance club and it also gives you height. Most players use this club extensively. Its distance is about 190 yards. Don't use the 3-wood in the rough unless you have a good lie. Most players go to the irons or a 4- or 5-wood in a situation like this. In long grass it is better to use an iron, because the grass has a tendency to tie up a wooden clubhead. The 4-wood, which has a distance of about 180 yards, is a good club to use when you have a long shot and have to clear trees or a water hazard. It gives you more loft. The 5-wood is a good club for bad lies and is easier to control than the irons. This is an exceptionally fine club for the woman golfer.

Uphill and Downhill Lies

In wood play, as well as in iron, it is important to know how to play uphill and downhill lies. For an uphill lie, first take a trial swing. It helps you determine where the clubhead will hit the ground. Use a less lofted club than normal. Keep the left knee bent a little more than usual. This helps keep your back level. Aim to the right to compensate for a probable hook. Play the ball forward of center.

On downhill lies, open your stance a bit and play the ball in back of center. Bend the right knee more than usual and more than the left knee. You should use a more lofted club than the shot actually calls for. Aim to the left to compensate for a probable slice. In both situations, uphill and downhill, always play the ball closer to the higher foot.

I R O N S

Width of Stance Varies

I cannot achieve a full pivot and correct weight transference if
my stance is too wide or if it is too narrow. It is, again, a
matter of comfort. When people ask me, "How wide should
my stance be?" I reply, "Wide enough to be comfortable."
With the woods, this width is usually the width of the
shoulders, or a fraction more, like mine. With the irons, it
will simply vary with each club. As the irons get higher
(2, 3, 4, etc.), I position my feet just a bit closer together and
open my stance.

Long Irons

When my game goes bad, I practice nothing but the 2-iron.
When I begin to hit well, I know my swing is back. There
is not much difference in my long-iron swing and my
swing with the driver. I am still trying to generate the most
power. Therefore, I concentrate mostly on keeping the
left wall strong. The swing, from beginning to end, is just
about the same except that my feet are a little closer together.

The 2-iron has very little loft. Maybe this is the reason
weekend golfers don't like it. In its place they go to the
3-wood or 3-iron. The 2-iron is good for about 180 yards. The
3-iron is more popular because it has extra loft. This means the
golfer can get the ball up better, and thus he has added

*My long-iron swing is the same as with the woods. I
still concentrate on keeping the left wall strong.*

confidence. The 3-iron has a maximum distance of about
170 yards.

You cannot baby either of these clubs; if you do, your shots
will be all over the course. Then you may be in the same
situation as a Scotsman I heard about. A man on a path near
the 17th hole at St. Andrew's suddenly ran through the
rough to the adjacent fairway and began yelling at a golfer
having trouble with the 2-iron.

"You blundering idiot," he shouted. "You almost hit my
wife just then."

"Oh, I say, I *am* sorry," replied the golfer. "Have a shot
at mine."

Medium Irons

In using the 4-, 5-, and 6-irons, you should not have as much
body turn as you do with the longer clubs. The distances
of these medium irons range from 160 yards with the 4-iron
to 140 yards with the 6-iron. Medium irons are fairly easy
to control and have the loft to put the ball in the air. As the
irons become shorter, move the ball back toward the right foot.
This allows you to hit down and through the ball without
problems.

It is important not to force medium irons. You cannot make
them do the same things as your long irons. But you must
also remember that you cannot baby these irons either. They
are accuracy instruments. The woods and the long irons
are your distance tools.

Short Irons

As my game becomes shorter, I open my stance more. Now I
want complete accuracy, not power. This is the only
time I am not concentrating strongly on the immovable left
side, because I am not going to hit the ball that hard.

With the short irons you have a shorter backswing than with
any of the other clubs. Because the clubs have shorter shafts
and because of the shorter backswings, you now move
the ball midway between the feet so you can get a good shot.

Your hands and arms are doing the work for you. Before,
the arms and legs did it. The short game takes much
practice. It is here that you can also cut many strokes off your
final score if you'll just have the patience to practice. One
of the most important factors in the short game is developing
a sense of feel. This will give you accuracy, timing, and
touch.

Chipping

Club selection is up to the individual and the situation.
Judgment, with both the club and the eye, is the key to a good
shot. You do most of your chipping with the 5-, 6-, and 7-irons.
Some use a 4-iron too. Chip shots usually are hit on a
low trajectory because you want them to roll as much as
possible.

For a chip shot, keep the feet fairly close together with the
weight on the left foot. The stance is slightly open. Pull
the left foot back from the target line. Play the ball from
opposite the center of the stance. Grip down on the club, near
the bottom of the leather. Keep the weight on the left foot
throughout. You will not have much wrist action. Keep
the hands slightly ahead of the clubhead. On impact,
concentrate on keeping the club coming through the ball.

In selecting the proper landing spot for the chip shot,
many golfers will read the greens the same way they would
for a putt. Accuracy counts here.

For a chip shot, the stance is slightly open with the weight on the left foot.

Play a pitch shot midway between the feet.

Pitch Shots

There is a definite distinction between the chip and pitch shots.
A chip shot assumes a lower trajectory because you are using
a less lofted club. Usually the player wants to land on the
green or just short of it. There is no backspin. Conversely, you
hit a pitch shot with a more lofted club. It carries high and
has backspin which brings it to a quick stop. Play this
type of shot at least midway between the feet. The backswing
goes only waist-high. The stance is open. The swing has
almost no wrist action.

IN TROUBLE

Keep Calm

A very serious gentleman approached me with a frown on
his face after shooting something like 18 over par and
said, "Chi Chi, I could have cut that score in half if it hadn't
been for the water hazards. What is the first thing you
do when you get in a water hazard?"

He was so serious, so intense, that I couldn't stop my
answer. "Look for alligators," I replied.

His reaction to water hazards and the other trouble spots
on the golf course was typical. The weekend golfer is
afraid of them. He lets them dominate his thoughts once he is
in the rough or sand or water.

The first rule to remember when in trouble is quite simple:
Just try to get out with a shot that will leave you in good
position to make up the lost ground.

Sand Shots

When you are in the sand, be it a fairway trap or one close
to the green, the first thing you must do is test the sand.
Always dig your feet into the sand to find out whether the base
is loose or, if it has rained, somewhat harder. Once you
have done this, plant your feet firmly, working them back
and forth until you have a solid hold in the sand. Use an open
stance for trap shots as well as all trouble shots. An open

*Always test the sand to find
out whether the base is loose
or strong.*

stance helps you bring the clubhead through against any extra
resistance like sand, water, or high grass.

The sand wedge is better than a 9-iron in these situations
because it has a heavy head and a thick bottom. The
9-iron has a lighter head. The wedge can cut into the sand
better.

On a short shot from dry sand, I hit an inch to two inches
in back of the ball. On a longer shot from wet sand I
would hit much closer. I don't crowd the ball and I usually
play it opposite my left foot. I concentrate on a slow
backswing. I swing completely through on these shots. There
can be no babying because the clubhead must cut through
the sand.

When you have a buried lie, close the clubface. Do not swing
too hard, but concentrate on following through. The ball
will come out easily enough. Don't make the mistake of
scooping the ball. The club is designed to do this for you, and
if you do scoop the shot you will not get a well-hit ball.

One of the most difficult of all sand shots is the downhill
lie. I play this off my right foot and I always allow for a roll
because the shot won't have any backspin. I again hit
an inch to two inches behind the ball. The movement of the
club is a sharp downward blow. I want to cut under the ball.

I don't crowd a sand shot, and I play it opposite my left foot. Swing completely through on these shots.

In the Rough

Now let's switch to the rough. The biggest problem here is that everyone tries to hit the ball as far away from the rough as possible. This means many golfers use a 3-wood instead of a 5-iron. I have explained before that it is better to use the irons in the rough because they cut through the grass much more easily than the woods.

Most players shoot bad rounds because they compound their difficulties in the rough. They gamble too much instead of just concentrating on getting the ball back on the fairway. Believe me, I've seen one golfer hit the same tree five times trying to get out of the rough.

Balls coming out of the rough will have top spin because you are hitting grass between the ball and the clubhead. So when you're shooting out of the rough you should remember that it is wise to use a more lofted club than, say, for a shot of the same distance on the fairway.

A lot of pros think that the physically strong golfer does better on shots from the rough than the smaller man. To a great extent this is true, but in the end it is the player who can generate the most clubhead speed who will come out of the rough in fine shape.

Water Hazards

In water, the main thing to remember is that you should try to
hit two inches behind the ball. This will compensate for
the club's skidding forward in the water. The clubface in this
situation is usually square. If the ball is more than two
inches deep, take the penalty and get out before doing your
score even more damage.

Purposely Hooking and Slicing

Other troublesome shots come when you have to hook or slice
on purpose to get around trees or to manipulate dog-leg
holes. To hook intentionally, turn both hands more to the
right than you normally would. Then close your stance. You
do this by stepping forward a little with the left foot.
You should aim more toward the right. This allows for the
curve of the ball from right to left. Slicing intentionally
is equally important. On this shot you turn both hands toward
the left, and this time you step back slightly with the left
foot. This makes you cut the ball from outside the line
of flight.

The main factor in my putting stance is keeping the weight on my left foot.

Putting Is a Barometer

Thinking positively is 90 per cent of the battle in putting. It's
a strange thing. When my putting is going well, usually
the rest of my game is too.

People tend to overlook my putting, because of the
emphasis on my long game. On the tour, though, nobody
underestimates me, because I have been known to make a few
dollars on the putting green from time to time.

The main factor in my putting stance is keeping the weight
on my left foot. This keeps me from losing my balance. I
also keep my eye on the back of the ball throughout the stroke.
I try to keep my head still and my body the same. As with
my other shots, I believe in putting fast. The guy who
dawdles is the guy who starts to get nervous, and the nervous
putter will miss.

On all putts, I read the break, step up to the ball, take one
look at the hole and one look at the ball, and stroke it.
I always try to make the stroke smooth and rhythmic, even
though I am taking little time over the ball.

A good lesson to learn in putting is never to see the ball
go into the hole, but to hear it. This is difficult, but by
practicing this way you will learn to keep your head down and
your body still throughout the stroke.

Always try to make the putting stroke smooth and rhythmic, even if you don't take much time over the ball.

Comfort First

As for the grip in putting, you should again experiment until you find the way that feels best for you. I prefer the reverse overlap grip. There is no one correct method of putting, however, and the worst thing many golfers do is to ruin what was a solid putting rhythm by useless experimentation. Experimentation is definitely necessary, but it can be overdone.

The best thing is to adopt the style you feel most comfortable with. Then practice with it until it becomes completely second nature. This, of course, includes the stance and swing.

Glancing at my stance, you will find that I am more pigeon-toed than the average person. This again is to steady my body. Most good putters won't lift a club more than an inch or two off the ground on the backswing. Golfers with exaggerated back strokes greatly increase the chances of error.

Reading the Greens

Reading the green is as important to your putting game as is
the stroke itself. You should become familiar with the
green the moment you step on it. First, see if it is hard. Check
to see if the grass is of fine texture or coarse. Determine
if the grass has recently been cut. Examine the grass around
the cup for its texture. You must do this on each hole.
If it is not your turn to putt, use the time to study the green
and your partner's shot. That way, you can benefit from
the roll his ball is taking and you can determine whether the
green slopes or not.

You must also determine whether the green is grainy or
not. When you are putting against the grain, you must hit the
ball harder. Grainy greens are those on which the grass
lies flat, not upright. When the sun is out, you can detect a
shine in the direction the grain runs. The ball will travel
much faster with the grain than against it. On courses near
water, the grain usually runs toward the water and
away from the mountains.

First Thoughts Are Best

After reading the green, you must determine the line of your shot. And remember, first thoughts are best. If you are having trouble confirming the line, go to the back of the hole and survey the scene from that position. If the putt is extremely long, go to a point equidistant from ball and hole. You should be able to find out if there is any slope from that spot. Once you have determined the line, then concentrate on it and nothing else. Get up to the ball, stroke it confidently, and you should have few problems. It's the second-guessers, the ones who make the scenes on the greens with all their tests, that usually wind up in the most trouble.

MENTAL ATTITUDE
AND PRACTICE

Practice Is the Key

Gary Player tells a great story about Jerry Barber that
should illustrate perfectly my point about practice. One time
Barber was practicing sand shots. Now, Barber is one of
the game's best sand players. He hit one ball near the
flag, and the next one went in. A kibitzer happened to be
watching Jerry and shouted, "Gee, you sure are a lucky
trap-shot player."

"Yes, I know," Jerry said. "And the harder I practice, the
luckier I get."

I've always liked that story because that's the way it is in
golf. At least it has been that way with me. I still practice
six or seven days a week. I've been doing it ever since I started
to play.

I remember when I was a kid I used to caddy and then
sneak out on the course late in the afternoon and play until
dark. I would play only between the 7th and 16th holes so I
wouldn't be caught. And do you know that my first clubs
were cut from guava trees and my first balls were made from
crushed tin cans?

I practice three hours a day when I'm not on tour. I start with the shorter clubs and work up to the woods.

Be Consistent

Right now I am still practicing about three hours a day
when I'm not on tour. Naturally, I concentrate on my long
game, but I don't neglect the rest. I usually start with
the wedge, then go to the 7-iron, the 5-iron, the 3-iron, the
3-wood, and the driver.

I don't put in too much time on the putting green because
to me putting has always been more of a mental thing
than anything else. Billy Casper is the perfect example of
this. He is considered one of the best putters on the tour, but
very seldom will you see him practicing it. I'm not saying
not to. I'm just trying to illustrate what I said in the
chapter on putting; it is 90 per cent mental.

So is the rest of golf. The trouble with the average golfer
is that he lets the game scare him. He reads this, he
reads that, and he doesn't know where to turn. I try to keep
things as simple as possible. I concentrate on the left wall,
speeding my legs, and making sure I have the proper
grip. People tell me I'm unorthodox, but I don't care when
my drives carry 300 yards.

Physical and Mental Conditioning

As for my physical conditioning, I do a lot of running —
a mile or so a day — and I do a lot of bar-bell exercises. In
fact, I used to do more than Gary Player, and he is known for
that. He even wrote a book about it. I also do isometrics.
I know the weekend golfer is not going to subscribe to
a regimen like that.

But there *is* time to practice. How many driving ranges are
there in the United States? Go out there, get a few buckets
of balls, and hit for a while at night after work. Not only
will it relax you, but it will make your game stronger.

Confidence is another important aspect of golf. I can tell
you to think positively, but in the end it is you who must
do it. You cannot let certain shots scare you. And the only way
to overcome this, if you really want to be a good golfer,
is to practice.

Practice at Home

If you are one of those people who have almost no time to practice, there are many things you can do around your home instead of going to the driving range or the country club. Simply gripping and swinging the club in the back yard is good exercise. Most sporting-goods stores sell plastic golf balls which do not carry far and therefore are ideal for practice with any club, provided you have a yard. The living-room rug makes a good putting green. (First be sure the "boss" doesn't mind.) If you are lucky enough to get to the course, then make sure your practice sessions accomplish something. They should have a specific goal. If they don't, you risk the chance of growing careless and sloppy.

Consult Your Professional

Go to your club professional whenever you feel your game is bad and getting worse. In most cases, he will spot what the trouble is and will help you correct it. But you must have confidence in him and you must be candid when he asks how much time you can devote to your game. You should also feel free to question him at any time; too many amateurs take advice without really knowing what they're hearing. At $15 per hour, that can be pretty expensive.

STRICTLY PERSONAL

I am glad I have finally finished this book. Now maybe all those people who see me on the professional tour will stop asking me how I hit the ball so far. They can satisfy their curiosity and make me a little more secure by buying the book.

Seriously, though, it is a big thing for me to have my own book. It is just another example of all the good things that have happened to me because of playing golf. I have built homes for my family, and to me the ability to do that is the most important gift I have received from the game.

Since I was a boy, my only goal has been to lift my family from the poverty I knew as a child. Now I have the opportunity, so you can understand why I don't mind all the time at the practice tee.

This is a personal trait: I have always been nervous because I work too hard. When I was younger, I worked with my father in the sugar fields. I dug ditches too, went to school, and caddied. I used to travel thirty-five miles from my home to the golf course, and since I started that I missed only one day of work. I remember going home at night but not being able to sleep because I had discovered something about my stance or swing and I wanted to go right out and practice it.

From my winnings as a professional, so far, I have built houses for two of my sisters and my mother. I am planning on building a house for my other sister. Then I will

Golf has been good to me. To have been able to build homes for my family is the most important gift I have received from the game.

build my own. This was always what I wanted to do. I never wanted to live better than my family.

Another goal is to take some of the poor boys in Puerto Rico and make good golfers out of them. Maybe what has happened to me could happen to them.

I plan, however, to cut down my time on the professional tour. I found in 1965 that I was getting extremely tired from playing so many tournaments in a row. There is a limit to the physical beating a person of my size can take. Walking six miles a day and practicing for a few extra hours becomes wearying. What I'll do this year is play three tournaments and then take a week off. It might improve things.

On the tour itself, I don't plan to change anything. I am Chi Chi Rodriguez and I don't care what the other pros say about my clowning. I want to give the gallery something for its money. When I make a putt or a good shot, I'm going to be happy and I'm going to show it. Without the galleries, there wouldn't be any tour. Right?

Some of the players, maybe five or so, complain about me, but I play better than they do and I have fun. Golf is still a game. I've got plenty of good jokes for the crowd. I tell them I can't decide if I look like Brando or Newman. They like that. They just like Chi Chi.

That's why it makes me sad when some of the pros criticize me. I've never tried to bother anybody. I just want the fans and pros to like me. If I can't stop bothering everybody by being the way I am, then I'm just going to quit and go home and teach all the kids in Puerto Rico how not to be poor. That would be a good life too.